THE ULTIMATE 10 Sports

CLUTCH PERFORMERS

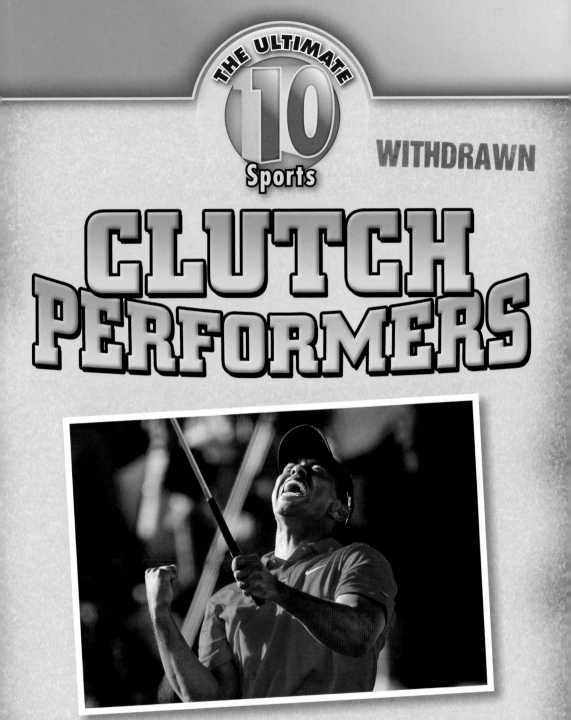

By Mark Stewart

Gareth Stevens
Publishing

Please visit our web site at www.garethstevens.com.
For a free catalog describing Gareth Stevens Publishing's list of high-quality books, call 1-800-542-2595 (USA) or 1-800-387-3178 (Canada). Gareth Stevens Publishing's fax: 1-877-542-2596

Library of Congress Cataloging-in-Publication Data available upon request from the publisher.
ISBN-10: 0-8368-9158-9 (lib. bdg.)
ISBN-13: 978-0-8368-9158-4 (lib. bdg.)

This edition first published in 2009 by
Gareth Stevens Publishing
A Weekly Reader® Company
1 Reader's Digest Road
Pleasantville, NY 10570-7000 USA

Copyright © 2009 by Gareth Stevens, Inc.

Executive Managing Editor: Lisa M. Herrington
Senior Editor: Brian Fitzgerald
Creative Director: Lisa Donovan
Senior Designer: Keith Plechaty
Photo Researcher: Kim Babbitt
Publisher: Keith Garton

Picture credits
Key: t = top, b = bottom
Cover, title page: Ross Kinnaird/Getty Images; pp. 4–5: Walter Iooss Jr./NBAE/Getty Images; p. 7: Andrew D. Bernstein/ NBAE/Getty Images; p. 8: (t) Andrew D. Bernstein/NBAE/Getty Images, (b) Nathaniel S. Butler/NBAE/Getty Images; p. 9: Mike Blake/Reuters/Corbis; p.11: Jeff Gross/Getty Images; p. 12: Timothy A. Clary/AFP/Getty Images; p. 13: Paul Mounce/Corbis; p. 15: Malcolm Emmons/US Presswire; p. 16: (t) Focus on Sport/Getty Images, (b) Mark Duncan/AP Images; p. 17: US Presswire; p. 19: Andrew D. Bernstein/NBAE/Getty Images; p. 20: (t) Andrew D. Bernstein/NBAE/Getty Images, (b) Dick Raphael/NBAE/Getty Images; p. 21: Rich Clarkson/NCAA Photos; p. 23: (t) Bettmann/Corbis, (b) Mark Rucker/Transcendental Graphics/Getty Images, p. 24: Mark Rucker/Transcendental Graphics/Getty Images; p. 25: B. Bennett/Getty Images; p. 27: Racing One/Getty Images; 28: Racing One/Getty Images; p. 29: Racing One/Getty Images; p. 31: Winslow Townson/AP Images; p. 32: Amy Sancetta/AP Images; p. 33: Ezra Shaw/Getty Images; p. 35: Nick Laham/ Getty Images; p. 36: Mark J. Terrill/AP Images; p. 37: Cameron Spencer/Getty Images; p. 39: Bruce Bennett Studios/Getty Images; p. 40: Ryan Remiorz/AP Images; p. 41: Ron Frehm/Ap Images; p.43 Noah K. Murray/The Star Ledger via US Presswire; p. 44: (t) Reuters/Corbis, (b) Mike Segar/Reuters/Corbis; p. 45: Timothy A. Clary/AFP/Getty Images; p. 46: (t) Jerry Wachter/NBAE/Getty Images, (b) AP Images.

Printed in the United States of America

1 2 3 4 5 6 7 8 9 10 09 08

Cover: Tiger Woods celebrates after sinking a clutch putt at the 2008 U.S. Open.

TABLE OF CONTENTS

Words in the glossary appear in **bold** type
the first time they are used in the text.

CLUTCH PERFORMERS

THE ULTIMATE 10 Sports

Welcome to The Ultimate 10! This exciting series highlights the very best from the world of sports.

Settle into your front-row seat to watch the greatest clutch performers in action. Feel the excitement build as these special athletes turn certain defeat into a thrilling victory. You may never watch sports the same way again!

In all sports, the difference between winning and losing can be razor-thin. Clutch performers live for those tense moments. These special athletes are the reason you never leave your seat until the final buzzer, the final out, or the final race.

This book tells the stories of 10 "ultimate" clutch performers. They stand out because they have been at their best when the pressure was greatest.

Michael Jordan of the Chicago Bulls shoots a jump shot against the New York Knicks in 1988. Jordan was never afraid to take the big shot at a key moment.

Under Pressure

Here are 10 athletes who rose to the top when the stakes were highest.

#1 Michael Jordan

#2 Tiger Woods

#3 Joe Montana

#4 Magic Johnson

#5 Babe Ruth

#6 Richard Petty

#7 David Ortiz

#8 Michael Phelps

#9 Mark Messier

#10 Derek Jeter

#1

Michael Jordan
A Legend Takes Flight

A great clutch player knows when to take control of a game. No athlete was better at this than Michael Jordan. His mind was constantly working. Jordan knew exactly when and how to make a difference in a close game. No one made more big plays than he did. When "His Airness" took flight, the game was usually as good as won.

FAST FACTS

NAME: MICHAEL JEFFREY JORDAN

BORN: February 17, 1963; Brooklyn, New York

COLLEGE: University of North Carolina

PRO TEAMS: Chicago Bulls, Washington Wizards

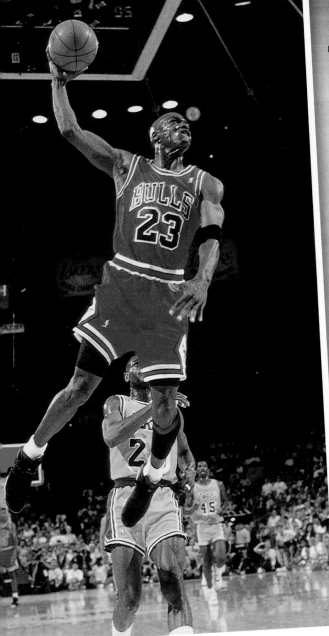

Michael Jordan soars for a dunk in 1991. That year, he led the Chicago Bulls to the first of six championships.

The Making of a Champ

Jordan was a good all-around athlete as a teenager. Still, he was cut from his high school basketball team as a sophomore. Jordan's intense desire to succeed made him practice even harder. He made the team in his junior year and averaged 25 points a game. As a senior, he was one of the best players in the nation.

Breaking Through

Jordan went to the University of North Carolina on a basketball scholarship. He played with great confidence in his first year. Coach Dean Smith chose Jordan to take the final shot in the 1982 championship game. With millions of fans watching, the 19-year-old swished a clutch shot to win the **NCAA championship**.

> **❝I've never been afraid to fail.❞**
> —Michael Jordan

Michael Jordan passes to Dennis Rodman during the 1996 NBA Finals. Teams focused on Jordan so much that his teammates got easy baskets.

Under Pressure

Jordan joined the Chicago Bulls of the National Basketball Association (NBA) in 1984. No player had ever made scoring look so easy. Yet Jordan didn't become a champion until he found ways to make his teammates better. He helped Scottie Pippen and Horace Grant become All-Stars.

In the 1997 NBA Finals, Steve Kerr won the final game with a jump shot. Jordan had the confidence to pass to his teammate for the winning basket. That gave Kerr the confidence to make it. With Jordan as their leader, the Bulls won six championships in the 1990s.

FOR THE RECORD

Jordan was the NBA's top scorer year after year. He was even more amazing in the playoffs. In 1986, he set a record with 63 points in a playoff game. In 1989, Jordan won a series against the Cleveland Cavaliers with a clutch shot in the final seconds. He averaged a record 41 points in the 1993 NBA Finals. No other player has scored more career points in the playoffs.

Which way will he go? Michael Jordan plans his next move during the 1993 NBA Finals.

Magic Moment

Jordan could win games at either end of the court. Sometimes, he won games at *both* ends. The Bulls faced the Utah Jazz in the 1998 NBA Finals. Late in Game 6, Chicago trailed by one point. Utah's Karl Malone moved in for the winning shot. But Jordan snuck in behind him and stole the ball.

Jordan dribbled up the court as the seconds ticked away. He put a great move on his man. Jordan then calmly hit a jump shot to win the championship. That famous shot was the last one he took for the Bulls.

Michael Jordan takes aim at the basket in the final seconds of the 1998 NBA Finals.

"I play to win, whether during practice or a real game."
—Michael Jordan

DID YOU KNOW?

Jordan was so good that he sometimes even amazed himself. The Bulls played the Portland Trailblazers in the 1992 NBA Finals. Jordan nailed six three-pointers in the first half of Game 1. After his sixth shot, Jordan looked to the crowd and shrugged. Not even he could explain how he got that hot!

#2
Tiger Woods
Always on the Prowl

The mark of a clutch athlete isn't always how he does against the competition. Sometimes it's how the competition does against *him*. Tiger Woods is so good that he forces other golfers to try difficult shots. He takes them "out of their game." When Woods has a lead in a tournament, he is almost impossible to catch.

FAST FACTS

NAME: ELDRICK "TIGER" WOODS

BORN: December 30, 1975; Cypress, California

COLLEGE: Stanford University

FIRST YEAR AS A PRO: 1996

Tiger Woods celebrates after making a clutch putt in the 2008 U.S. Open. He always wears red in the final round of a tournament.

The Making of a Champ

Tiger Woods picked up his first golf club before age 2. He won his first world championship at age 8. By the time he was a teen, Woods was beating adult golfers. He learned to play from his father. Earl Woods did not just teach his son how to swing. He also taught Tiger the mental toughness to play his best under pressure.

> **The ultimate goal is to be the best.**
> —Tiger Woods

Breaking Through

Woods became the country's youngest U.S. Junior **Amateur** champion at age 15. Three years later, he became the youngest Amateur champion. He won both titles three times. At 20, Woods won the 1996 NCAA championship.

FOR THE RECORD

Golf has four major tournaments, or majors. They are the Masters, the U.S. Open, the British Open, and the PGA Championship. Here is how Tiger Woods compares with other legends in golf's four major events.

GOLFER	WINS	FIRST WIN	LAST WIN
Jack Nicklaus	18	1962	1986
Tiger Woods*	14	1997	2008
Walter Hagen	11	1914	1929
Gary Player	9	1959	1978
Ben Hogan	9	1946	1953
Tom Watson	8	1975	1983

* Through 2008

A crowd watches as 21-year-old Tiger Woods makes history at the 1997 Masters.

Under Pressure

Woods left college to turn pro at the end of the 1996 season. Golf fans expected a lot from him. How would he do against the best golfers in the world? Woods answered that question at the 1997 Masters. He won the tournament by an incredible 12 strokes. He shot a record 18 under **par**. Within months, he was the top-ranked golfer in the world. No golfer had ever been so good so young. Over the next decade, Woods only got better.

Tiger Woods carefully studies a putt in the playoff round of the 2008 U.S. Open. His great focus makes him a top clutch performer.

Magic Moment

Woods has had many amazing victories. His most remarkable win came at the 2008 U.S. Open. Woods was playing with a painful leg injury. At the end of the third round, he made two **eagles** and chipped in a **birdie**. In the final round, Woods made a clutch 12-foot putt on the last hole. That forced an 18-hole playoff with Rocco Mediate.

At the end of the playoff round, Woods made another amazing putt. He forced a **sudden death** playoff. He finally defeated Mediate on the next hole. Two days later, Woods had surgery to fix a torn knee and fractured leg!

> **"He beat everybody on one leg!"**
> —Golfer Kenny Perry, after Woods won the 2008 U.S. Open

DID YOU KNOW?

Through 2008, Woods had entered the final round of a major tournament in first place 14 times. He won every one of those tournaments!

#3

Joe Montana
Football's Mr. Cool

Too skinny. Too weak. Too slow. When Joe Montana joined the National Football League (NFL), few experts thought he would become a star quarterback. The football world soon discovered that Montana may have been too *good*. He took over a bad San Francisco 49ers team and turned them into Super Bowl champions.

FAST FACTS

NAME: JOSEPH CLIFFORD MONTANA JR.

BORN: June 11, 1956; New Eagle, Pennsylvania

COLLEGE: University of Notre Dame

PRO TEAMS: San Francisco 49ers, Kansas City Chiefs

The Making of a Champ

Montana's best sport as a teenager was basketball. He led his high school team to the state championship. He was **recruited** to play for the powerful North Carolina Tar Heels. Montana chose to play football for Notre Dame instead. Fans of the Fighting Irish were glad he did. In one of his first games, he led Notre Dame to an amazing comeback against—you guessed it—North Carolina!

Breaking Through

Montana led his team to one great victory after another. In his final college game, Notre Dame beat the University of Houston 35–34. The win came on the last play of the game. In 1979, the San Francisco 49ers **drafted** Montana. They hoped he would do for them what he had done for Notre Dame.

Joe Montana looks for an open receiver. By staying calm when others panicked, Montana was able to make clutch throws his whole career.

> **"I always felt, within myself, I can find a way to win."**
> —Joe Montana

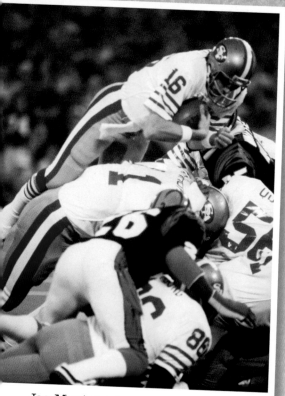

Joe Montana leaps over several Cincinnati Bengals and into the end zone in his first Super Bowl.

Under Pressure

Montana turned the 49ers into the top team in the National Football Conference (NFC). In his first year as a starter, he guided the team to the NFC Championship Game. His touchdown pass to Dwight Clark in the final seconds won the game. Next, Montana led the 49ers to their first Super Bowl victory. He was named Super Bowl Most Valuable Player (MVP).

Three years later, San Francisco went 15–1 and won another Super Bowl. Montana was the MVP again. In all, he led the team to four Super Bowl wins.

FOR THE RECORD

Montana was at his best when the games counted most. He set NFL postseason records with 5,772 passing yards and 45 touchdown passes. Montana is the only player to be named Super Bowl MVP three times. In four Super Bowls wins, Montana did not throw a single interception. In Super Bowl XXIV, he threw for five touchdowns. Three of them went to his favorite receiver, Jerry Rice. The 49ers destroyed the Denver Broncos 55–10.

Joe Montana high-fives a teammate after a touchdown in Super Bowl XXIV.

Joe Montana's eyes light up during Super Bowl XXIII. He made great passes during tense moments of big games.

Magic Moment

The test of a true clutch quarterback comes when a championship is on the line. Montana passed that test in Super Bowl XXIII against the Cincinnati Bengals. Cincinnati was ahead 16–13 with 3:10 left in the game. The 49ers had the ball on their own 8-yard line. They were 92 yards away from a score.

"Joe Cool" marched his team down the field. He calmly picked the defense apart with passes to Roger Craig and Jerry Rice. Montana threw a touchdown pass to John Taylor to win the game with 34 seconds left.

❝If every game was a Super Bowl, Joe Montana would be undefeated!❞

—Former teammate
Randy Cross

DID YOU KNOW?

In the NFL, Montana led his team to 31 comeback wins. The 49ers erased a 35–7 lead by the New Orleans Saints in 1980. In 1989, Montana threw for four fourth-quarter touchdowns in a comeback win over the Philadelphia Eagles.

#4

Magic Johnson
Nice Guys Finish First

During the 1980s, the Los Angeles Lakers treated fans to a fast-paced brand of basketball they called "Showtime." The man who made the Lakers go was Earvin "Magic" Johnson. He was a player like no other. Magic could do anything he set his mind to—and always seemed to be having fun. He was all smiles on the court. But when a game was in doubt, Magic was all business.

FAST FACTS

NAME: EARVIN "MAGIC" JOHNSON

BORN: August 14, 1959; Lansing, Michigan

COLLEGE: Michigan State University

PRO TEAM: Los Angeles Lakers

Magic Johnson floats past a pair of Boston Celtics during a 1983 game. Johnson was a guard, but he had the size and skill to play any position on the court.

The Making of a Champ

As a child, Earvin Johnson didn't go anywhere without a basketball. People knew he was coming by the sound of the bouncing ball. He lit up gyms all over Michigan with his dribbling and passing skills. His smile could light up a room. A sportswriter nicknamed him "Magic" in high school. Everyone who saw him play knew the name was perfect.

Breaking Through

At age 17, Magic led Everett High School to the state championship. Two years later, he led Michigan State University to the NCAA championship. Magic played at a time when most point guards stood about 6 feet tall. He towered above them at 6 feet 9 inches. Basketball had never seen anything like him.

"I never think that there's something I can't do."
—Magic Johnson

FOR THE RECORD

The NBA had two "Kings of Clutch" during the 1980s. Johnson was one. His friend and rival, Larry Bird, was the other. They first met in the 1979 NCAA Championship Game. Johnson led Michigan State to a win over Bird and Indiana State. The pair continued to battle after Bird joined the Boston Celtics. Bird and Magic met in the NBA Finals three times during the 1980s.

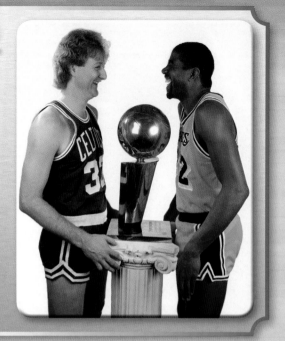

Under Pressure

Johnson joined the Los Angeles Lakers for the 1979–1980 season. During the 1960s and 1970s, the Lakers had reached the NBA Finals nine times. They had "won it all" only once. Magic changed that. The bigger the game, the better he played. He could beat teams with his scoring, his passing, or his rebounding.

Magic led the Lakers to the NBA Finals nine times. They won five championships. He was named NBA Finals MVP in three of those series.

Magic Johnson dribbles around Kareem Abdul-Jabbar. They led the Lakers to five NBA championships.

Magic Moment

Lakers center Kareem Abdul-Jabbar was injured in Game 5 of the 1980 NBA Finals. Coach Paul Westhead asked Magic to start at center in Game 6. A **rookie** guard playing for a 7-foot 2-inch superstar? The experts said the Lakers were in deep trouble.

L.A. fans had no need to worry, though. Magic not only played center but forward and guard, too! The Philadelphia 76ers did not know how to guard him. Magic scored 42 points and had 15 rebounds and seven **assists**. The Lakers beat the 76ers 123–107 to win the championship.

The Philadelphia defense is helpless against lightning-quick Magic Johnson in the 1980 NBA Finals.

"I have always looked up to him because he knows how to win."

—Larry Bird, on Magic Johnson

DID YOU KNOW?

Magic left the NBA in 1991 after learning he had HIV, the virus that causes AIDS. After receiving treatment, he returned to play in the 1992 All-Star Game. He scored 25 points and was named MVP.

21

#5

Babe Ruth
A Two-Way Terror

The World Series is baseball's ultimate pressure cooker. Some of the game's best hitters and pitchers have flopped in the Fall Classic. Until a player stands on the mound or steps into the batter's box, he doesn't know how he will react. Babe Ruth pitched *and* hit like a champion in the World Series. No other athlete loved the big stage as much as he did!

FAST FACTS

NAME: GEORGE HERMAN "BABE" RUTH

BORN: February 6, 1895; Baltimore, Maryland

DIED: August 16, 1948; New York, New York

PRO TEAMS: Boston Red Sox, New York Yankees, Boston Braves

The Making of a Champ

Young George Ruth was a wild child. He spent much of his boyhood in reform school. There he taught himself how to play baseball. Ruth threw and swung as hard as he could. Opponents laughed at the teenager when he arrived in the major leagues with the Boston Red Sox. They thought "the Babe" played baseball like a little kid.

Babe Ruth watches one of his long blasts sail to the outfield. He was the first great slugger in baseball.

Breaking Through

Ruth had the last laugh. He soon became one of the best pitchers in baseball. In the 1916 World Series, he pitched a 14-inning victory. Two years later, he hurled a 1–0 shutout in Game 1 of the World Series. He also won Game 4. In all, Ruth pitched 29⅔ innings in a row without giving up a run!

Babe Ruth shows the form that made him a star pitcher for the Red Sox.

Babe Ruth (right) discusses hitting with teammate Lou Gehrig. The fearsome Yankees lineup was nicknamed "Murderers' Row."

Under Pressure

In 1920, Ruth joined the New York Yankees. He had given up pitching by then. He was too good a hitter to sit on the bench. Ruth became the biggest celebrity in the country. Fans packed into ballparks to see him. Other athletes might have hated all the attention. Ruth loved it.

He played in seven more World Series after joining the Yankees. New York won championships in 1923, 1927, 1928, and 1932 with Ruth starring in right field.

FOR THE RECORD

Babe Ruth was the ultimate "fall" guy. When the weather cooled in autumn, his bat heated up. Here is how Ruth compared with other Yankees legends in World Series play.

PLAYER	AT BATS	HOME RUNS	RUNS BATTED IN	BATTING AVERAGE
Babe Ruth*	118	15	30	.347
Lou Gehrig	119	10	35	.361
Joe DiMaggio	199	8	30	.271
Yogi Berra	259	12	39	.274
Mickey Mantle	230	18	40	.257

*Ruth's numbers are with the Yankees only.

Babe Ruth launches a long home run in Game 3 of the 1932 World Series. It was his 15th career home run in the World Series.

Magic Moment

Ruth's last World Series was in 1932, against the Chicago Cubs. His legs ached and his bat was slow, but he was still a great showman. He loved to give fans a thrill. In Game 3, Ruth hit a three-run homer in his first at bat. As he batted in the fifth inning, the Cubs tried to distract him. They yelled insults. Ruth yelled right back and pointed toward center field. Moments later, he blasted a long homer to center field. Did Ruth "call his shot"? Baseball fans are still arguing about that today!

DID YOU KNOW?

One of Ruth's most embarrassing moments happened in 1926 against the St. Louis Cardinals. He was caught stealing in Game 7 to end the World Series. In 1928, Ruth got his revenge. He blasted three home runs against St. Louis in Game 4 to help the Yankees sweep the series.

#6

Richard Petty
King of the Road

Race-car drivers are fearless by nature. It takes a lot to make them sweat. During the 1960s and 1970s, there was no scarier sight than Richard Petty's number 43 car coming up from behind. Petty was auto racing's ultimate clutch driver. All he cared about was crossing the finish line first. Petty believed that every race was his to win. He was right 200 times!

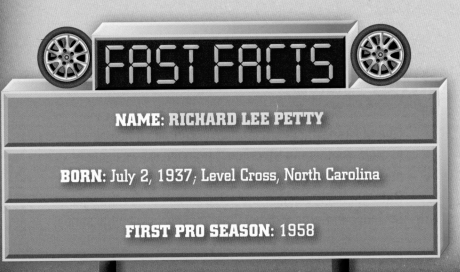

FAST FACTS

NAME: RICHARD LEE PETTY

BORN: July 2, 1937; Level Cross, North Carolina

FIRST PRO SEASON: 1958

Richard Petty speeds around the track at the 1974 Daytona 500. He went on to win the race for the fifth time in his career.

The Making of a Champ

Petty learned his craft working under the hood of his father's car. Lee Petty was one of the superstars in the early days of stock-car racing. In 1959, Lee won the first Daytona 500. It was—and still is—the most important race in **NASCAR**. Later that year, Richard was named NASCAR Rookie of the Year.

> **" In the good old days you had to be more than good. You had to be tough *and* good. "**
>
> —**Richard Petty**

Breaking Through

In 1967, Petty had the greatest season in history. He took the checkered flag 27 times. Petty won races in every possible way that year. He won some by racing way ahead of the field. He won others on the last lap. Sometimes it seemed as if the other drivers were just "waiting" for Petty to win.

FOR THE RECORD

There's a reason Richard Petty was called "the King." Here is how he compares with other members of racing "royalty."

ACHIEVEMENT	RICHARD PETTY	DAVID PEARSON	DALE EARNHARDT	JEFF GORDON*
NASCAR Championships	7	3	7	4
Daytona 500 Wins	7	1	1	3
Top 10 Finishes	712	366	428	336
Victories	200	105	76	81

*Through 2008

Richard Petty celebrates his win at the Daytona 500 in 1981. It was his seventh victory in the big race.

Under Pressure

After Petty's great 1967 season, fans began to call him "King Richard" or simply "the King." He earned that title by out-driving the competition at speeds of close to 200 miles per hour. All NASCAR drivers need to be fearless, but Petty was also smart. He knew when to lay back and when to stomp on the gas pedal. More than any other driver, he loved the pressure of a big race.

The King of NASCAR never missed a race, either. From 1971 to 1989, he made 513 starts in a row!

Richard Petty makes a pit stop during the 1979 Daytona 500. The exciting race helped make NASCAR much more popular.

Magic Moment

For many years, NASCAR was considered a Southern sport. That changed in 1979. That year, the Daytona 500 was shown on national TV for the first time. Millions watched as Petty lurked behind the two leaders until the final lap. When their cars spun out, Petty surged past them. In a wild finish, he took the checkered flag just ahead of Darrell Waltrip. The King had won his sixth Daytona 500. His amazing clutch performance helped win over countless new NASCAR fans.

> **"I don't think anyone is going to be the next Richard Petty."**
> —NASCAR driver Jeff Gordon

DID YOU KNOW?

Petty won his 200th and final race in 1984. President Ronald Reagan was in the stands. No president had ever attended a NASCAR race before. After the race, Reagan joined Petty and his **pit crew** to celebrate.

#7

David Ortiz
Every Out Is Precious

The Boston Red Sox have had many powerful hitters over the years. None could deliver the clutch hits needed to win championships. That changed when David Ortiz joined the team in 2003. "Big Papi" has more big hits in more big games than anyone playing today. Along the way, he ended years of suffering for Boston fans. Ortiz has been a manager's dream—and a pitcher's worst nightmare!

FAST FACTS

NAME: DAVID AMÉRICO ORTIZ ARIAS

BORN: November 18, 1975; Santo Domingo, Dominican Republic

PRO TEAMS: Minnesota Twins, Boston Red Sox

The Making of a Champ

Every young baseball player has an idol growing up. For Ortiz that person was his father, Enrique. Enrique taught his son that every out is precious to a hitter. As young David grew into a fearsome slugger, he never forgot that lesson.

Breaking Through

David reached the major leagues with the Minnesota Twins. The Twins saw that Ortiz had the makings of a great clutch hitter. The team was not sure that he could stay injury-free, however. The Boston Red Sox swooped in and signed Ortiz in 2003. Minnesota's loss was Boston's gain. He hit 31 home runs and drove in 101 runs that summer.

David Ortiz watches a long ball sail toward the right-field stands at Fenway Park.

"If you go up there thinking you might not get it done, you're out already."

—David Ortiz, on why hitters need confidence

Under Pressure

What a start! David Ortiz connects for a three-run home run in his first World Series at bat in 2004.

With Ortiz in the lineup, Boston was a different team. The Red Sox had not won a championship since 1918. Their fans had grown used to disappointment. Ortiz gave fans a reason to believe that a championship was within reach.

In 2004 and again in 2007, Ortiz led the team to victory in the World Series. As a bonus to Red Sox fans, he did his best hitting against the hated New York Yankees.

FOR THE RECORD

For hitters, the pressure builds when runners are on second and third base. Ortiz loves those situations. When he bats with runners in scoring position (RISP), his average soars!

SEASON	HOME RUNS	RUNS BATTED IN	OVERALL AVG*	WITH RISP**
2003	31	101	.288	.273
2004	41	139	.301	.350
2005	47	148	.300	.352
2006	54	137	.287	.288
2007	35	117	.332	.362
2008	23	89	.264	.336

*Batting average   **Batting average with runners in scoring position

Magic Moment

Ortiz was at his best in the 2004 American League Champions Series (ALCS). The Red Sox lost the first three games to the Yankees. Boston was one defeat away from the end of their season. In Game 4, Ortiz hit a game-winning home run in the 12th inning. In Game 5, he hit home run in the eighth inning. Ortiz came up with a man on base in the 14th inning. He fouled off eight two-strike pitches. He then hit a bloop single to drive in the winning run. Ortiz homered in Game 7 to help Boston win the **pennant**. He was named MVP of the series.

David Ortiz celebrates after winning Game 4 of the 2004 ALCS. He would have even more big hits later in the series.

DID YOU KNOW?

Ortiz had one of his best clutch seasons in 2005. He hit 20 home runs that either tied the score or gave the Red Sox the lead.

#8

Michael Phelps
Strokes of Genius

Is there such a thing as a "clutch" swimmer? At the 2008 Olympics, Michael Phelps entered eight events, and he promised eight gold medals. He delivered on that promise against the best swimmers on the planet. It doesn't get more clutch than that! Phelps ruled the pool while the whole world was watching. His pressure performance ranks among the greatest in sports history.

FAST FACTS

NAME: MICHAEL FRED PHELPS

BORN: June 30, 1985; Baltimore, Maryland

COLLEGE: University of Michigan

Michael Phelps competes in the 200-meter butterfly at the 2008 Olympics.
He had set his first world record in the event seven years earlier.

The Making of a Champ

Phelps began racing at age 7. He was not a natural. In fact, he didn't even like to put his face in the water! By age 11, however, he was on his way to becoming a champion. His coach Bob Bowman told Michael's parents that their son could be an Olympian. In 2000, Phelps made the U.S. team and competed in the 200-meter butterfly.

Breaking Through

Phelps started setting world records in 2001. He was just 15 years old! His first record came in the 200-meter butterfly.

> **❝I love to race the best people in the world.❞**
> —**Michael Phelps**

In 2002, he set a record in the 400-meter individual **medley**—a race in which a swimmer uses four different strokes. At the 2003 World Championships, Phelps set five world records.

FOR THE RECORD

In 1972, Mark Spitz set a record with seven Olympic gold medals. In 2008, Michael Phelps beat that record by one. Here is how the two swimming legends compare.

EVENT	MICHAEL PHELPS	MARK SPITZ
400-meter Individual Medley	World Record	—
200-meter Individual Medley	World Record	—
200-meter Freestyle	World Record	World Record
200-meter Butterfly	World Record	World Record
100-meter Butterfly	Olympic Record	World Record
100-meter Freestyle	—	World Record
400-meter Freestyle Relay	World Record	World Record
800-meter Freestyle Relay	World Record	World Record
400-meter Medley Relay	World Record	World Record

Michael Phelps raises his arms after winning the 100-meter butterfly at the 2004 Olympics.

Under Pressure

By 2004, Phelps was ready for the greatest stage—the Olympics. He won six gold medals and two bronze medals. Phelps kept setting new records over the next few years.

He set his sights on the 2008 Olympics in Beijing, China. Phelps placed the ultimate pressure on himself: He said he wanted to win a gold medal in all eight events. The eyes of the world focused on him as the Summer Games began.

Magic Moment

Winning eight gold medals was not easy. Phelps had some scary moments along the way. The first came in the 400-meter freestyle relay. Phelps and his teammates needed a record-setting swim by Jason Lezak to win gold. In the 200-meter butterfly, Phelps's goggles filled with water. He set a new world record anyway!

In the 100-meter butterfly, Phelps was behind until the last stroke. He made one last lunge and won by one one-hundredth of a second. His final race was the 400-meter medley relay. It was Phelps's eighth gold and his seventh world record.

Michael Phelps (right) celebrates his team's win in the 400-meter freestyle relay at the 2008 Olympics.

❝The guy thinks there's nothing he can't do.❞
—U.S. swimmer Nate Dusing

DID YOU KNOW?

At the 2004 Olympics, Phelps gave up his spot on the 400-meter medley relay team before the final race. He wanted his friend Ian Crocker to have a chance to win a gold medal. The U.S. team won, and Crocker got his gold.

#9
Mark Messier
Man on a Mission

It takes a special player to win six hockey championships. It takes a crazy player to guarantee a victory. Mark Messier was a little of both. By 1994, he was already one of the best clutch players in history. Then he promised New York a win in the playoffs. After he delivered that victory, Messier became a sports legend.

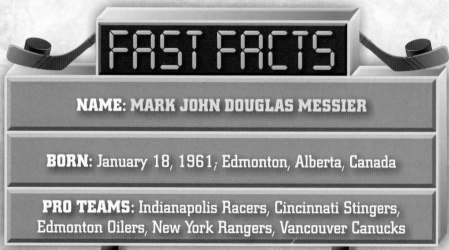

FAST FACTS

NAME: MARK JOHN DOUGLAS MESSIER

BORN: January 18, 1961; Edmonton, Alberta, Canada

PRO TEAMS: Indianapolis Racers, Cincinnati Stingers, Edmonton Oilers, New York Rangers, Vancouver Canucks

Mark Messier scans the ice for an open teammate. He was talented, tough, and one of the great leaders in sports history.

The Making of a Champ

At age 11, Messier was a skinny stick boy for a minor-league hockey team. Five years later, he was the star of that same team. By the time he was 21, Messier was a 50-goal scorer in the National Hockey League (NHL). Messier did everything well on the ice. Soon he would become a great leader, too.

> **The only pressure I'm under is the pressure I've put on myself.**
> —Mark Messier

Breaking Through

In 1984, Messier helped the Edmonton Oilers win the Stanley Cup. He won the Conn Smythe Trophy as the MVP of the playoffs. Still, Messier played in the shadow of teammate Wayne Gretzky, hockey's greatest player. They won three more Stanley Cups together. In 1988, the Oilers traded Gretzky. Messier became the team captain.

Under Pressure

In 1990, Messier won the Hart Trophy as the league MVP. He led the Oilers to a fifth championship. Hockey fans finally realized what a clutch player he was.

Messier joined the New York Rangers in 1991–92. The team had not won a championship since 1940. The pressure was on Messier to bring the team a Stanley Cup. In his first year, he was named MVP again. In 1993–94, the Rangers finished with the league's best record. Messier then set his sights on the Stanley Cup.

Mark Messier proudly lifts the Stanley Cup in 1990. It was his fifth championship with Edmonton.

FOR THE RECORD

Mark Messier was at his best in the playoffs. He was equally good at scoring goals and setting up teammates with great passes. Here are his numbers from the six years he led his team to the Stanley Cup.

YEAR	GAMES	GOALS	ASSISTS
1983–84	19	8	18
1984–85	18	12	13
1986–87	21	12	16
1987–88	19	11	23
1989–90	22	9	22
1993–94	23	12	18

Magic Moment

The Rangers met the New Jersey Devils in the 1994 playoffs. The winner would go to the Stanley Cup Finals. The Devils led the series three games to two. Before Game 6, Messier guaranteed a victory. New York was behind by two goals in the third period. Then Messier took over. He scored a **hat trick** to win the game. No one could remember a better performance in such a high-pressure situation.

New York faced the Vancouver Canucks in the 1994 Stanley Cup Finals. Once again, Messier was "the Man." His goal was the difference in Game 7. Messier and the Rangers were NHL champions.

Mark Messier scores the first of his three goals against the New Jersey Devils in Game 6 of the 1994 playoffs.

> **❝In any form of competition or battle, he is the perfect leader.❞**
> —Former teammate Mike Richter

DID YOU KNOW?

Clutch players do not always make great leaders. Messier was both. In 2006, the NHL created the Mark Messier Leadership Award in his honor.

#10

Derek Jeter
Mr. November

When baseball teams need a win, they usually look to muscle-bound sluggers or flame-throwing pitchers. For more than a decade, the New York Yankees have looked to Derek Jeter. His quiet confidence and upbeat attitude make him a great leader. His competitive fire makes him one of the most feared big-game players in sports.

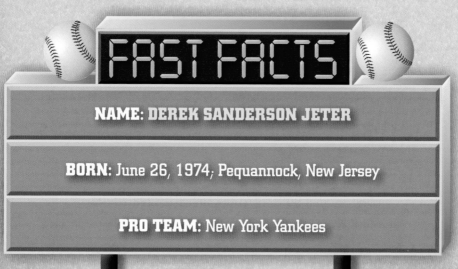

FAST FACTS

NAME: DEREK SANDERSON JETER

BORN: June 26, 1974; Pequannock, New Jersey

PRO TEAM: New York Yankees

Derek Jeter slaps a base hit to right field. In 2008, he set a record for the most career hits at Yankee Stadium.

The Making of a Champ

Baseball came naturally to Jeter as a child. Still, he was always trying to get better. No matter how good the competition, he wanted to test himself against the best. The Yankees gave him that chance. In 1992, the team drafted Jeter out of high school. By 1995, he was playing in the big leagues. Jeter became New York's starting shortstop in 1996. He hit his first career home run on Opening Day.

> **"I never think about my own stats, as long as I'm contributing to the team."**
> —Derek Jeter

Breaking Through

The 1996 Yankees were a team of tough **veterans**. Jeter was just 21, but he fit right in. He batted .361 in the playoffs and led the team in runs scored in the World Series. He earned his first of four championship rings that fall.

Derek Jeter hits a first-inning home run in Game 4 of the 2000 World Series.

Under Pressure

Baseball games often come down to one important play. Time and again, Jeter has been a part of those clutch moments. In the 1998 playoffs, he hit a key two-run triple that helped the Yankees win the pennant.

In the 2000 World Series, the Yankees played the rival New York Mets. Jeter homered in the last two games and was named MVP. In the 2001 playoffs, he saved the Yankees' season with his defense. He made an amazing play that cut down a runner at home plate.

FOR THE RECORD

In baseball, statistics tell only part of the story. Jeter's toughness and dedication are what truly make him a special player. In 2004, he made an incredible play against the Red Sox. Late in the game, Jeter raced toward the foul line to catch a pop-up. He caught the ball and then dove face-first into the seats. Jeter was bloody and bruised, but he still made the out! Fans voted it the play of the year in an online poll.

Alex Rodriguez (#13) and fans cheer as Derek Jeter makes his amazing diving catch in 2004.

Magic Moment

One of Jeter's finest moments came during Game 4 of the 2001 World Series. The game was played on October 31. The season had been delayed by the terrorist attacks of September 11. New Yorkers needed something to cheer about.

The Yankees and the Arizona Diamondbacks were locked in an extra-inning battle. At midnight, the scoreboard flashed: "Welcome to November Baseball." Moments later, Jeter walked to the plate. He drove a pitch into the stands for the winning home run. The stadium erupted as Jeter circled the bases. A fan held up a sign that said it all: MR. NOVEMBER.

Derek Jeter rounds the bases after his game-winning home run in the 2001 World Series.

66 **There's just something about him. When he's on the field, good things happen.** 99
—Former teammate Aaron Boone

DID YOU KNOW?

In 2000, Jeter became the first player to be named MVP of the All-Star Game and the World Series in the same year.

Honorable Mentions

Larry Bird
Pro Team: Boston Celtics

If there was a smart way to win a basketball game, Larry Bird was sure to find it. He was a great shooter and passer. But he also did the "little things" that gave his team an edge. Bird always seemed to be in the right place at the right time—for a rebound, a loose ball, or a steal. He led the Boston Celtics to three NBA championships in the 1980s and was named NBA MVP three times. His rivalry with Magic Johnson energized the NBA.

Otto Graham
Pro Team: Cleveland Browns

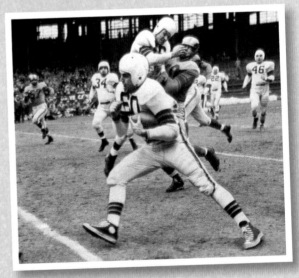

Clutch quarterbacks lead their teams to championship games. No one did that better than Otto Graham. He played 10 seasons for the Cleveland Browns and led them to the championship game in each season. In his final game, in 1955, the Browns beat the Los Angeles Rams 38–14. It was Cleveland's seventh NFL championship with Graham as its quarterback. Graham was a winner even before he joined the NFL. In 1946, he won a league title with the Rochester Royals of the old National Basketball League.

Glossary

amateur: an athlete who does not receive a salary. High school and college players are considered amateurs.

assists: passes that lead to successful shots

birdie: a hole completed in one stroke under par. A golfer who finishes a par-4 hole in three strokes has birdied that hole.

drafted: chose a college player to join a professional team

eagles: holes completed in two strokes under par. A golfer who finishes a par-5 hole in three strokes has eagled that hole.

hat trick: the feat of scoring three goals in one game

medley: a swimming race that includes four different strokes—backstroke, breaststroke, butterfly, and freestyle

NASCAR: the National Association for Stock Car Auto Racing. A stock car is shaped like a car found "in stock" at an auto dealership.

NCAA championship: the honor won at the end of a season by the top athlete or team in a college sport. *NCAA* stands for *National Collegiate Athletic Association.*

par: the number of strokes a golfer is expected to take to finish a hole. A golfer is expected to take four strokes to finish a hole that is par 4.

pennant: a league championship. The pennant winners of the American League and the National League meet in the World Series.

pit crew: members of a racing team who work on a car during refueling stops

recruited: offered a scholarship by a college team

rookie: a player in his or her first season as a professional

sudden death: a way of deciding the winner of a game or match that is tied. In golf, the first golfer to make a better score on a sudden-death playoff hole is awarded a victory.

veterans: players with a lot of experience

For More Information

Books

Garner, Joe. *And the Crowd Goes Wild.* Naperville, Ill.: Sourcebooks MediaFusion, 2002.

Herzog, Brad. *The 20 Greatest Athletes of the 20th Century.* Sports Illustrated for Kids Books. New York: Rosen Publishing, 2002.

Stewart, Mark. *The Chicago Bulls.* Team Spirit. Chicago: Norwood House, 2007.

Web Sites

Major League Baseball
mlb.com

National Basketball Association
www.nba.com

The Pro Football Hall of Fame
www.profootballhof.com

Publisher's note to educators and parents: Our editors have carefully reviewed these web sites to ensure that they are suitable for children. Many web sites change frequently, however, and we cannot guarantee that a site's future contents will continue to meet our high standards of quality and educational value. Be advised that children should be closely supervised whenever they access the Internet.

Index

About the Author

Mark Stewart is the "ultimate" clutch sports author. He has filed stories on one-hour deadlines and set up workstations under stadium staircases. Mark wrote the first book about Tiger Woods, *Tiger By the Tale*. He was hired the day Woods won the 1997 Masters and had to finish the book in 15 days. Fortunately, not every book is a buzzer beater. For *Clutch Performers*, Mark was allowed to take his time.